THE YOUNG MESSIAH

BOB DARDEN

FOREWORD BY MAX LUCADO

SPARROW PRESS

NASHVILLE, TENNESSEE

Published 1994 in Nashville, Tennessee, by Sparrow Press, and distributed in Canada by Christian Marketing Canada, Ltd.

Printed in the United States of America

98 97 96 95 94   5 4 3 2 1

Library of Congress Cataloging-in-Publication Data:

Darden, Bob, 1954–
        The young Messiah   / Bob Darden.
                p.   cm.
        ISBN 0917143426 : $14.95 ($24.95 with CD insert)
        1. Contemporary Christian musicians—Interviews. 2. Concerts—
        United States. 3. Handel, George Frideric, 1685–1759. Messiah.
        I. Title.
        ML394.D35 1994
        782.5' 06' 073   dc20

                                                                94–35036

                                                                    CIP

All Scripture quotations are from The Holy Bible, King James Version.

Art Direction: Karen Philpott

Design: Barnes & Co.

Photographs: Russ Harrington & Paul Natkin

THE
YOUNG
Messiah

Contents

Foreword

MAX LUCADO

The Young Messiah celebrates two events that no one noticed.

To see the first, go to a cave in Bethlehem. To see the second, a studio in London. In the first a mother struggles to give birth. In the studio a composer labors to do the same. The mother's name is Mary. The composer? George Frideric Handel.

Handel is writing music for what he intends to be his final concert. The year is 1741. He is in debt. His music hasn't sold. His future is bleak. He has every intent of abandoning his career in music.

But what a career it has been. No one was more successful than young Handel. From Germany to Italy and finally to London, the masterful musician left a trail of genius. But after 25 years the public's taste has changed and with it changed Handel's fortune.

Health failing and money gone, he has resolved to quit. But before he can, he has one more obligation. A friend by the name of Charles Jennings has given him a text based on the life of Jesus. Jennings suggests Handel put it to music.

Handel might have resisted had he not at the same time been offered a commission from the Dublin charity to compose a work for a benefit concert.

The message was of Christ. The purpose was for the poor. How could Handel refuse?

So on August 22, 1741, he retires to his small house on Brook Street and begins to work.

Great compositions require time.

Brahms needed 23 years to complete his first symphony . . .

Rachmaninoff spent 27 years writing and rewriting his Piano Concerto No. 1 . . .

Even Beethoven took 18 months to compose his only opera . . .

But from start to finish Handel writes *Messiah* in 24 days! The musician is consumed by the experience. He writes as if under a spell. He does not leave his house; he allows no visitors to disturb him. He ignores food brought by servants. He doesn't sleep and rebuffs anyone who urges him to rest. His servants speak of the wild fury in his eyes and fear that he is losing his mind.

For three weeks and three days he dwells in another world. A realm where rhythm and tone are supreme. A realm in which he sees God. A servant finds him sobbing as he composes.

After completing the Hallelujah Chorus he states, "I did think I did see heaven before me, and the great God himself." To a friend he confesses, "Whether I was in the body or out of my body as I wrote it I know not." And to his physician he confides, "I think God has visited me."

The result of that August in London is the greatest oratorio in history.

But London had no idea.

While Handel worked the city passed by unaware. Business folk carried on the work. Salesclerks sold their wares. People walked back and forth in front of the house on Brook Street unaware of the miracle occurring within.

We seldom see a miracle when it happens. They didn't see it in London and they didn't in Bethlehem.

People in Bethlehem were like the people in London. Too busy to imagine the incredible. Too busy to notice the couple who had come the night before. Too preoccupied to be concerned about the young pregnant girl. Even the keeper of the inn had more important things to do than clear out a room for this carpenter and his wife.

After all, there was work to be done.

So while Bethlehem worked, Mary and Joseph arrived. While Bethlehem slept, the Messiah was born.

Have things changed since Bethlehem? Are people different than they were in London? Do we notice the remarkable when it happens?

Seldom. But such is the purpose of Christmas—to remind us of the incredible.

And such was the experience of Handel—he saw God.

And such is the hope of *The Young Messiah*—that you may see what Mary saw, that you may hear what Handel heard and that you may rejoice that God has come into your world.

Introduction

GEORGE FRIDERIC

HANDEL: MAESTRO

OF MESSIAH

DR. PATRICK KAVANAUGH

If Handel's father had had his way, the Hallelujah Chorus would never have been written. His father was a "surgeon-barber"—a no-nonsense, practical man who was determined to send his son to law school. Even though young Handel showed extraordinary musical talent as a child, his father refused for several years to permit him to take lessons.

George Frideric was born in 1685, a contemporary of Bach, a fellow German, and was raised a fellow Lutheran, yet they were never to meet.

When Handel was eight or nine years old, a duke heard him play an organ postlude following a worship service. The boy's father was summarily requested to provide formal music training for him. By the time Handel turned 12, he had written his first composition and was so proficient at the organ that he substituted on occasion for his own teacher.

Young Handel continued through the years to master the clavichord, oboe and violin, as well as composition. In 1702 he entered the University of Halle to study law—out of respect for his late father's desire. But he soon abandoned his legal studies and devoted himself entirely to music.

He became a violinist and composer in a Hamburg opera theater, then traveled to Italy from 1706 to 1710 under the patronage of their music-loving courts. In Rome, Handel wrote "The Resurrection," an oratorio in which religious themes emerged for the first time in his music. While in Italy, Handel met some of the eminent musicians of his day, notably Domenico Scarlatti.

In 1712, after a short stay at the court of Hanover, he moved to England, where he lived for the rest of his life. There he anglicized his name from its original spelling, "Georg Friedrich."

Like his fellow composer Bach, Handel was renowned as a virtuoso organist. One Sunday, after attending worship services at a country church, Handel asked the organist's permission to play a postlude. As the congregation was leaving the church, Handel began to play with such expertise that the people reclaimed their seats. The regular organist finally stopped him, saying that Handel had better not play the postlude after all, if the people were ever to get home.

Although he wrote his greatest music in England, Handel suffered personal setbacks there as well. Falling in and out of favor with changing monarchs, competing with established English composers, and dealing with fickle, hard-to-please audiences left him confronting bankruptcy more than once.

Audiences for Handel's compositions were unpredictable, and even the Church of England attacked him for what they considered his notorious practice of writing biblical dramas to be performed in secular theaters. His occasional commercial successes soon met with financial disaster, as rival opera companies competed for the ticket holders of London. He drove himself relentlessly to recover from one failure after another, and finally his health began to fail. By 1741 he was swimming in debt. It seemed certain he would land in debtor's prison.

But then the miracle intervened, and he composed in 24 days the most celebrated choral music in human history—*Messiah*.

One of Handel's many biographers summed up the consensus of history about his masterpiece: "Considering the immensity of the work, and the short time involved, it will remain, perhaps forever, the greatest feat in the whole history of music composition."

Messiah premiered in Dublin on April 13, 1742, as a charitable benefit, raising 400 pounds and freeing 142 men from debtor's prison. A year later, Handel staged a performance in London, attended by the King of England himself. As the first notes of the triumphant "Hallelujah Chorus" rang out, the king rose from his seat. Following royal protocol, the entire audience stood too, initiating a tradition that has lasted for more than two centuries.

Soon after, Handel's fortunes increased dramatically, and his hard-won popularity remained constant until his death. By the end of his long life, *Messiah* was firmly established in the standard repertoire. Its influence on other composers would be extraordinary. When Haydn later heard the "Hallelujah Chorus," he wept, exclaiming, "[Handel] is the master of us all!"

> "*Messiah's music and message has probably done more to convince people there is a God than all the theological works ever written.*"

Handel conducted more than thirty performances of *Messiah*. Many of these concerts were benefits for the Foundling Hospital, of which Handel was a major benefactor. The money Handel's performances of *Messiah* raised for charity led one biographer to note: "*Messiah* has fed the hungry, clothed the naked, fostered the orphan . . . more than any other single musical production in this or any other country." Another wrote, "Perhaps the works of no other composer have so largely contributed to the relief of human suffering."

Messiah changed Handel's life, as well as the lives of thousands who have heard the composition. Testimonies abound of those who gave their lives to Christ through experiencing the spiritual intensity of this masterpiece. One biographer stated that *Messiah's* music and message "has probably done more to convince people there is a God than all the theological works ever written." For its composer, it served as a turning point that eventually led to his sustained success and the universal recognition of his genius.

Handel was a devout follower of Christ and widely known for his concern for others. At church he was often on his knees, praying with "the utmost fervor of devotion." Handel's morals were above reproach, and he was known for his modest and straightforward opinion of himself and his talent. When a friend unwittingly commented on the dreariness of the music he had heard at the Vauxhall Gardens, Handel replied, "You are right, sir, it is pretty poor stuff. I thought so myself when I wrote it."

His friend Sir John Hawkins recorded that Handel "throughout his life manifested a deep sense of religion. In conversation he would frequently declare the pleasure he felt in setting the Scriptures to music, and how contemplating the many sublime passages in the Psalms and contributed to his edification."

Known universally for his generosity and concern for those who suffered, Handel donated freely to charities even in times when he faced personal financial ruin. He was a relentless optimist whose faith in God sustained him through every difficulty.

As Handel's life drew to an end, he expressed his desire to die on Good Friday, "in hopes of meeting his good God, his sweet Lord and Savior, on the day of his resurrection." He lived until the morning of Good Saturday, April 14, 1759. His death came only eight days after his final performance, at which he had conducted once again his masterpiece, *Messiah*.

His close friend James Smyth wrote of Handel, "He died as he lived— a good Christian, with a true sense of his duty to God and to man, and in perfect charity with all the world." Handel was buried in Westminster Abbey with over 3,000 attending his funeral. A statue erected there shows him holding the manuscript for the solo that opens part three of *Messiah*, "I know that my redeemer liveth."

Since its creation, universal popularity of Handel's *Messiah* has skyrocketed. It is performed each year in every major city in the world. There are hundreds of *Messiah* recordings, and the text has been translated and sung in dozens of languages. It is in the standard repertoire of virtually each chorus in the world, and there are many organizations that exist solely for the performance of Handel's *Messiah*.

Its genius shines forth through a variety of modern interpretations. Today there are danced *Messiahs*, folk *Messiahs*, even a hula *Messiah*. *The Young Messiah* is another in a long line of creative offspring of the original created over two-and-one-half centuries ago.

Handel wanted his masterpiece, *Messiah*, "to make people better," to bring them closer to God, to give them a true encounter with the *Messiah*, Jesus Christ. Whether through the original version or *The Young Messiah*, the music's ultimate message is the same: May all who experience this message proclaim with George Frideric Handel "I know that my Redeemer liveth!"

PARTIALLY EXCERPTED FROM
*THE SPIRITUAL LIVES OF
GREAT COMPOSERS,*
BY PATRICK KAVANAUGH.
© 1991 SPARROW PRESS.
ALL RIGHTS RESERVED.
USED BY PERMISSION.

> *H*andel donated freely to charities even in times when he faced personal financial ruin.

14

A Contemporary

Messiah Evolves

There are dozens upon dozens of versions of Handel's *Messiah* in print, each "new" in that no absolutely definitive, universally accepted version of the score has ever been uncovered. With each performance during his lifetime, Handel added or subtracted voices or instruments or even changed the score to match individual voices. In addition to the "irreverent" new syncopations, certain vocalists and instrumentalists were actually paid extra for their improvising skills. Consequently, the first performances of *Messiah* in Dublin were markedly different than those Handel conducted in London for the Foundling's Hospital in his later years.

Even those who produced *Messiah* in the years to come—most notably Mozart—added their own distinctive stamp to the already heavily annotated scores.

And when the rage for massive choruses began in England in the nineteenth century and swept into the United States in the twentieth century (the latest incarnation being the "Sing-Along *Messiah*" trend of the 1980s), those elements too were added to the public's perception of the "proper" production of *Messiah*.

All of this melding and adapting of the original music may horrify purists and mystify musicologists, but it probably befits a work that itself is a masterful blend of different styles: English church music (especially in the choruses), the ancient German Passion-music tradition, the Italian melodic style (three of the choruses are arranged from Italian love duets Handel had written thirty years earlier!), and of course grand opera.

The end result is a particularly organic piece of music, one of the few in the entire classic library pliable enough—and sometimes resilient enough!—not only to endure for 250-odd years, but to flourish under generations of innovations, additions, subtractions and interpretations.

As soon as sound recording progressed beyond the primitive stages, Handel's *Messiah* was an early addition to the classical catalogs. It has remained in print ever since, in literally hundreds of versions, from 78 to vinyl to cassette to compact disc.

Legendary Christian composer (and *Young Messiah* conductor) Ralph Carmichael is generally credited with recording the first of the "new," rock-oriented *Messiahs*. "So far as changing the musical style, I have no problem with that," Carmichael said. "About fifteen years ago, I did a film score for Billy Graham called *His Land*. They wanted something unusual for the final sequence. So I said, 'Let's take the Hallelujah Chorus and do all the traditional lines, except that under everything we'll record a rock rhythm section.'"

Fortunately for posterity, the producers agreed with Carmichael's revolutionary concept.

Because of the overt Christian message of the text, it wasn't long after that the new contemporary Christian music labels began to pay close attention to the *Messiah*. One of the earliest versions was *Messiah* (Birdwing Records and Tapes BWR 2011), a four-record set released in 1979.

Sparrow Records president Billy Ray Hearn, who continued a lifelong attraction to Handel's masterpiece, served as executive producer of the project. The recording featured the London Philharmonic Orchestra and the London Philharmonic Choir, conducted by John Alldis. Irving Martin produced the project, which was recorded in All Saints Church in London.

Sparrow also released *Christmas Portion of Handel's Messiah* (Birdwing BWR 2027) that year. This version contained the entire Christmas story of the Gospels, excerpted from the Birdwing production.

Then came the *Young Messiah* by The New London Chorale (Myrrh MSB-6658), also in 1979. The project was the brainchild of English artist Tom Parker, then a 35-year-old self-taught composer/arranger/producer. In

1973 he scored a #1 pop hit with a rock version of "Jesu, Joy of Man's Desiring," which he retitled "Joy." Parker then released several albums featuring rock treatments of music by Bach, Mozart, Beethoven, and Tchaikovsky, before 1979's *Young Messiah*.

This *Young Messiah* didn't sell particularly well. But among those who heard it was a young English musician named Norman Miller. Miller was thrilled with the concept but not with the execution. In 1990, Miller convinced Word Records to return to the contemporary Messiah concept and release what he called *Handel's Young Messiah* (Word 7019132502). Miller's team featured religious music veterans Paul Mills and Don Hart as producers and arrangers, Barry McGuire as narrator, and a number of well-known contemporary Christian artists singing the solos, including Matthew Ward, First Call, The Imperials, Sheila Walsh, Russ Taff, Wayne Watson, Annie Herring, Twila Paris, Whiteheart, Cynthia Clawson and Phil Driscoll.

It was this version, along with several of the artists from the record, that Miller took on the first *Young Messiah* tour.

In 1992, Reprise/Warner Alliance (9 26980-2) released *Handel's Messiah, A Soulful Celebration*. A host of well-known African-American artists, producers, arrangers and musicians joined the project. Norman Miller was involved again, and was joined as co-executive producer by Gail Hamilton and Mervyn Warren.

The lineup of artists participating included Vanessa Bell Armstrong, Daryl Coley, Lizz Lee, Chris Willis, Mike E., Dianne Reeves, Patti Austin, Tramaine Hawkins,

> *Even those who produced Messiah in the years to come—most notably Mozart—added their own distinctive stamp to the already heavily annotated scores.*

Howard Hewitt, Stevie Wonder, Take 6, Sounds of Blackness, The Boys Choir of Harlem, Leaders of the New School, Michelle Weeks, The Richard Smallwood Singers, The Yellowjackets, Commissioned, The Clark Sisters, Al Jarreau and Tevin Campbell.

The climactic Hallelujah Chorus boasted a who's-who of African-American artists. In addition to most of the performers listed above, the "Hallelujah" choir featured Andrae Crouch, Sandra Crouch, Clifton Davis, Larnelle Harris, Edwin Hawkins, Chaka Khan, Gladys Knight, Babbie Mason, Johnny Mathis, Marilyn McCoo, Stephanie Mills, Jeffrey Osborne, David Pack, Phylicia Rashad, Joe Sample, Thomas Whitfield, Vanessa Williams, Bob Bailey and a host of others.

Handel's Messiah, A Soulful Celebration was one of the best-selling releases of 1992 and won numerous industry-wide awards as well.

Finally, in 1993, Sparrow released *The New Young Messiah* (SPD 1404) to immediate public and critical acclaim. Miller took virtually the entire cast intact on tour in November and December of 1993, where it set a number of attendance records across the country, outdrawing some of the best-known names in American popular music.

Today it is one of the largest-grossing concerts series of the year—and has been for the past four consecutive years.

Today it attracts a galaxy of stars from the contemporary Christian music firmament, a Who's Who of artists of faith.

Today, in the largest cities in America, with a full choir and orchestra, with state-of-the-art lights and sound, with exclusive pay-per-view airings, with videos and CDs and cassettes and striking merchandise, *The Young Messiah* is an unparalleled evening of sacred music.

This book is the story of the people behind the tour and music of *The Young Messiah.*

Chapter *1*

WAYNE WATSON

"COMFORT YE MY PEOPLE"

Wayne Watson

Comfort ye, comfort ye my people, saith your God. Speak ye comfortably to Jerusalem, and cry unto her, that her warfare is accomplished, that her iniquity is pardoned . . . The voice of him that crieth in the wilderness, Prepare ye the way of the Lord, make straight in the desert a highway for our God.

– Isaiah 40:1-3

OPENING *THE YOUNG MESSIAH* with the gentle ballad "Comfort Ye" and selecting Wayne Watson to sing it are twin strokes of genius.

Watson is one of the most respected and revered figures in contemporary Christian music. Through songs like "Home Free," "Friend of a

Wounded Heart," "Watercolour Ponies," "Touch of the Master's Hand," a shelf full of Dove Awards, and an uncompromising stand on artistry and integrity, Watson has quietly assumed a leadership position in the industry.

And rather than being a brassy and attention-grabbing opener, arranger David Hamilton crafted "Comfort Ye" into a gentle, peaceful introduction to a work of unsurpassed beauty and power. By placing it first, the creators of *The Young Messiah* are saying, in effect, "The music is nice—but what matters is the Message."

It's a statement that Watson strongly agrees with.

"`Comfort Ye My People' is gentle and comforting," he said. "The beauty of *Messiah* is the marriage of the music to lyric. It puts people at ease.

"The audience we draw for *Young Messiah* is mixed. There are serious believers and there are others who were brought by family or friends saying, `Come on, let's have Christmas.' But deep in the hearts of everybody, what they wish and pray for is peace in their homes and—most of all—in their own hearts. They pray for comfort. These lyrics say to them, `Relax, be at ease.'"

It's a message that Watson believes people are craving today.

"People need to hear that more than ever," he said. "And that's what `Comfort Ye My People' is about. It's a lot broader theologically than that, but as far as a down-to-earth, personal application, that's the crux of it.

"I like the song because it is not a showpiece, but a preparatory piece to the rest of the work. I enjoy that role of preparing the audience for what is to come. That's the role I've always played and I don't mind it."

Going first before a new, unknown audience has been likened to batting lead-off against the opposition's ace fireballer. You take all the heat. But Watson likes taking the point, even in an evening full of instrumental and vocal highlights and fireworks.

"From a performance standpoint, I do enjoy going first—then I'm through for the evening," he said with a laugh. "But with the upcoming tour, I'll be more involved because they've added two more songs for me to sing!"

But don't fret for Watson—he says the added numbers are a joy, not a burden. And that joy is readily apparent in every note he sings.

"By the time I get up to sing, the song is really a part of me," he said. "I don't want to split my attention thinking about what note or what word comes next.

"At the same time, to be honest, I don't always concentrate on the audience, either—I try to have a vertical perspective. Sometimes it is almost embarrassing that people are watching me. I recently read a statement by an old-time preacher who wished he could preach behind a veil so that people wouldn't be distracted by his delivery. All they could do was listen to his message.

> "Deep in the hearts of everybody, what they wish and pray for is peace in their homes and—most of all—in their own hearts."

"Maybe in contemporary Christian music we've gone too far the other way. Our facial nuances and expressions have become an integral part of what we do. I think sometimes that can distract from the supernatural elements of the work. I'm trying to find that place right in the middle. Performing and entertaining are both part of it—but there is a much, much bigger element to what and why we sing—and I'm trying to focus on that element."

Obviously, in Watson's case, it is working. It is one of the reasons that he has been a staple of the *Young Messiah* tours.

"I've always gone with the conviction that I'm to be a cheerful

helper, an encourager—whatever is needed most on tour," he said.

And Watson adds more than a strong, facile voice to *The Young Messiah's* already impressive lineup. In an industry that sometimes seems obsessed with youth, he's become both a spokesperson and someone the other artists go to when they need someone to listen.

"I've been around since 1980, and like it or not, that makes me one of the old guys," he said. "The audience and other artists tend to watch you a little closer because you *are* one of the old guys. That means you do some counseling of the younger artists and you answer their questions.

"**A**nd the fellowship with the other artists is one of the most enjoyable aspects of the tour. It's great to spend concentrated time on the road with the other guys."

"*Messiah* is timeless," he said. "The fact that it has stayed alive all these years says something. The Lord has used this work like few pieces that have ever been written. As a writer, I am amazed at the complexity of it—but it is still simple enough for everyone to digest.

"Handel obviously was inspired to write it; time has proven that. When it is sung at Christmas or Easter, the most important thing is that it always points our attention to the reason we're celebrating.

"That's the beauty of it."

> "**I** recently read a statement by an old-time preacher who wished he could preach behind a veil so that people wouldn't be distracted by his delivery. All they could do was listen to his message."

Chapter 2

26

LARNELLE HARRIS

"Ev'ry Valley Shall Be Exalted"

Larnelle Harris

Every valley shall be exalted, and every mountain and hill made low; the crooked straight, and the rough places plain.

– Isaiah 40:4

FOR MORE THAN A QUARTER OF A CENTURY, Larnelle Harris has embodied contemporary Christian music. After twenty-five years of inspired number-one singles ("I Can Begin Again," "The Father Hath Provided," "I Miss My Time With You," "I've Just Seen Jesus" and others), five Grammy Awards, ten Dove Awards, and just about every other honor religious music has to offer, he continues to stand as a shining example of what's right with this industry.

He's also one of only three artists (besides Sandi Patty and Ralph Carmichael) who has been on every *Young Messiah* tour.

"(Executive producer) Norman Miller called out of the blue to ask me to be part of the first tour," Harris said. "After he named all of the artists who were involved, I said, 'Let me think about it . . . That's enough time. OK!' And I've been on every tour since.

"*Young Messiah* seems to have caught the attention of everyone. The crowds are phenomenal, the spirit is phenomenal. Because of all the artists, we have Sandi fans, Larnelle fans, Ralph Carmichael fans, all coming together. It creates an atmosphere of praise and worship.

"I have good memories of all the tours. Nothing has changed over the years except the musical arrangements. The spirit certainly hasn't changed."

And like his fellow artists, what Harris cherishes most has been the intimate time with other singers and musicians.

"Before the *Young Messiah* tours, we didn't get to spend much time together," he said. "But on the tour, for instance, we share a devotional time each night, with different ones leading. They might share a particular problem that only another artist can relate to, and we all pray together.

"After a few nights of that, you go out to sing not with nine or ten artists but with nine or ten friends. And you know who is having trouble singing these songs that night, and you're pulling for them, praying for them, to get through."

Harris said that the *Young Messiah* tours have done more to break down barriers among artists than any other single event. And after twenty-five years in the business, he should know!

"Being together on tour has eliminated any competition," he said. "That's what happens when Christians get together, share together, pray together, live together.

"And the result is that when we meet at industry meetings or other events, it is like running into a brother or sister. You want to get in a corner together and talk and catch up. *The Young Messiah* tours create that kind of closeness."

The end result is a remarkably focused group of women and men working towards the same goal—a leveling kind of humility and consistency in their lives. As the song says, "Every valley shall be exalted, and every mountain and hill made low; crooked straight, and the rough places plain."

"The gospel does that, for my God causes all things to work together for his glorious purpose," Harris said. "And it doesn't matter if things are joyful or sorrowful. You don't have to worry about that because the Lord gives us an evenness, a consistency in our lives no matter what the circumstances."

But Harris said the words of Isaiah 40:4 say something else to the discerning listener: "They say that I don't have to give up. Sometimes people give up. They throw up their hands and cry, 'What's the use?' But Christians know that all things work together for good. We know from verses like this that it is never too late to pray. The Bible says, 'They shall call on my name, and I will hear them: I will say, 'It is my people.'

> "*Being together on tour has eliminated any competition. That's what happens when Christians get together, share together, pray together, live together.*"

"And finally, these words remind me that bad and good times will come to us all. That makes the words to this song easier for me, a black man in a white society, to sing. If I wanted to waste my time, I could be angry about a lot of things. But the Lord evens that out. He helps me to love those who are unlovable and he helps me to be lovable.

"'Every valley shall be exalted, and every mountain and hill made low.' You can't go under him, you can't go over him. In Psalm 148, David sang that *everything* must praise the Lord—and that he affects everything. You have to believe that."

"Ev'ry Valley Shall Be Exalted" is one of the showpieces of *The Young Messiah*. Mervyn Warren's arrangement sends Harris's booming voice through an array of impressive vocal acrobatics, much like the featured singers of Handel's time. Harris, whose multioctave voice is a true treasure of contemporary Christian music, handles it with his usual grace.

But amid the improvisations and impressive vocals, there is a serious, life-changing message. And if you watch Harris sing "Ev'ry Valley," you can see it in his face.

> "*S*ometimes people give up. They throw up their hands and cry, 'What's the use?' But Christians know that all things work together for good."

"What's going through my mind while I'm singing this song? I'm thinking of the people out there listening. Some don't know the Lord, some are riding on the last pew, and some are fervent and call upon the Lord every day. Every time I sing this song, I'm saying to them with all I've got that the Lord works in everything! In every valley! On every mountain! Everything is taken care of! He makes it all work, and you can trust him!

"And sometimes as I sing I think this may be the last time I get to share this message with that one person out there—so I want it to be the clearest expression of that thought possible."

One of Harris's best-loved songs is the moving, convicting "I've Just Seen Jesus."

Likewise, Handel exclaimed upon completing the mighty "Hallelujah Chorus," "I did think I did see all Heaven before me, and the great God Himself."

George Frideric Handel and Larnelle Harris—now *that's* something worth singing about in every valley and from every mountain top!

Chapter 3

SANDI PATTY

"And the Glory of the Lord"

Sandi Patty

And the glory of the Lord shall be revealed, and all flesh shall see it together; for the mouth of the Lord hath spoken it.

Isaiah 40:5

TO MANY PEOPLE, Sandi Patty epitomizes contemporary Christian music. More than her gold and platinum albums, more than her truckloads of Grammy and Dove Awards, she's shown that you can be featured on virtually every major network television show without compromising your Message.

She was, then, a logical choice to serve as the first host of the mammoth *Young Messiah* tours, a role she's held from the beginning with grace, charm and unflappable good cheer.

And because of her glorious multi-octave voice, Executive Producer

Norman Miller and the show's various producers and arrangers have called on her to sing more and more. On the recorded version of *The Young Messiah,* she sings "And the Glory of the Lord" and duets with Steven Curtis Chapman on "He Shall Feed His Flock." And on tour, she's just as likely to be found singing in other trios and quartets as well.

> "It struck me that *Messiah* really is a complete spiritual journey. It is the story of our faith."

"And the Glory of the Lord" was tailor-made for Patty. Arranged and orchestrated by Alan Moore, it is a soaring power praise/ballad requiring exquisite control. Patty's voice surges effortlessly over the full choral accompaniment but is never showy or frivolous. The notes are there. She hits them beautifully. No mean feat, incidentally. Ask any arranger.

It's obvious every moment she's on the stage, whether singing or reading the narration or serving as host, that Sandi Patty is doing something she loves.

"'And the Glory of the Lord' in the original *Messiah* is a full chorale piece," Patty said. "When they asked me to sing it as a solo, I said, `Well, OK—but there's going to have to be some real creativity here.' But arranger Alan Moore really is that creative and I love this version.

"And one of the things I love about it is that even if you didn't hear the words, if you only heard the music, you'd get the essence of the song. That's because the majestic music reveals so much about the nature of God. It is powerful, upbeat and a nice blend of lyric and melody. It is also in keeping with the emotion of the original version."

Patty, who was a precocious college student when she sang the soprano arias in *Messiah* with the San Diego State Chorale and Symphony, says she ultimately has come to regard the entire composition as a praise proclamation.

"It struck me that *Messiah* really is a complete spiritual journey," she said. "It is the story of our faith. It starts with the creation, goes through the rise of humankind, the birth of Jesus, his life, Resurrection and Second Coming. Musically and spiritually it has much to offer.

"I thought it was daring for Norman Miller to attempt to keep the integrity of *Messiah* but update it musically so that people who shy away from classical music would find it more accessible. There probably were some musical purists out there who saw this as sacrilege. But because of the positive way it has been received from the beginning, I think people sense that this contemporary restyling is faithful to the original intent of *Messiah*."

Not surprisingly, when Miller assembled the team to record the original *Young Messiah* album, Sandi Patty was atop the list of artists he wanted.

"After a few tour dates to great crowds—and once word got out what a great time we were having touring together—Norman's phone started ringing off the hook with artists saying, 'Hey, Norm, how about keeping me in mind for next year?' The wonderful response that first year really surprised us all."

When the public embraced *The Young Messiah* concept from the beginning, Patty said both the organizers and critics were taken aback at the outpouring of love and support for the project.

"First, I don't think they were expecting such timely music with such an incredible story," she said. "Second, there was real interest in see- ing that many artists coming together. It's like going to see the World Fig- ure Skating Tour—with all of your favorite skaters together on one rink!"

And, for the artists themselves, having that many fellow artists together for an extended period of time was appealing.

"Most of us never have the opportunity to spend that kind of time together," Patty said. It's a rare privilege to be together.

Despite all of the vocal and instrumental pyrotechnics and the awe-inspiring music on stage, Patty says many of her best memories have come offstage: on the bus rides, in the hotels, talking backstage or having dinner with a new friend.

"I have incredibly fond memories of all of the tours," she said. "The people, every one of them on all of the tours, have been fun, insightful, challenging, merciful, kind and gracious.

"**A**s you can imagine, everybody is in a different place spiritually and emotionally. Some are struggling at the same time that others are experiencing an exciting mountain-top year. It has been neat to get know each other—and to try to find what the others need. You don't have that kind of opportunity to share deeply when you only see somebody twice a year at industry functions. With *The Young Messiah* tours, we got to spend time together on the bus, at breakfast, just hanging together. Those are times I'll always remember."

Fortunately for the audience, Patty's times onstage have been just as memorable. "And the Glory of the Lord" is a genuine showstopper, but Patty modestly gives credit to Handel's inspired use of Scripture.

"The verse I'm singing is one of the proclamations of prophets," she said, "telling the world that very soon the glory of the Lord—Jesus—will be revealed and all flesh will see it together. I take that to mean that even if you haven't been paying attention, you're not going to miss it! We've all felt the impact of the glory of the Lord being revealed in the course of history since Jesus was born.

"A lot of the prophets used phrases like *and the mouth of the Lord hath spoken* to say that 'This is not my word—this is the word of the Lord. I'm just a messenger. And the message is the glory will be revealed for all to see. So be it. That's the way it is!'

"To me, this is a statement about a power that is going to be felt for the rest of time."

The ancient Jews believed that the glory that surrounded God was so powerful that you almost couldn't speak of it, Patty said.

"And that was what was in the Ark of the Covenant, that glorious, mysterious, unutterable presence of God that you're in awe of and in fear of at the same time.

"The prophet is saying that once that glory is revealed, we will all comprehend it. It is a glory and power that is not stuck away in a box somewhere. Rather, this is the glory of the Lord revealed for all flesh to see it together, to the remotest part of the world.

"As I sing the words, I can almost feel them resonating!" said Patty.

Interestingly, when Sandi Patty sings those words, audience members report feeling that resonance as well.

But they call it *goose bumps*.

Chapter 4

STEVEN CURTIS CHAPMAN

"BUT WHO MAY ABIDE THE DAY OF HIS COMING"

Steven Curtis Chapman

But who may abide the day of his coming, and who shall stand when he appeareth? For he is like a refiner's fire.

– Malachi 3:2

THE CHOICE OF STEVEN Curtis Chapman for the *Young Messiah* tour was obvious. He's still the same aw-shucks, modest guy he was when he was hoofin' and singin' eight times a day at Opryland.

But he also has clearly emerged as one of contemporary Christian music's premier artists. And, he was asked to sing two songs on *The New Young Messiah*, a duet with Sandi Patty titled "He Shall Feed His Flock," and the moving solo "But Who May Abide the Day of His Coming?"

Surprisingly, Chapman—a noted homebody and family man—found that he enjoyed life on the road with the *Young Messiah* cast and crew:

"Probably one of the best ways to sum it up is to tell you that this is the only tour where my wife said, `Look: I really want you to go. Do this—it's important—because I know how much it means to you. You get to have fellowship with the guys and you come back refreshed and excited. But even though it is hard for you to be gone right before Christmas—I encourage you to do it.'

"That says a lot—if you knew my wife, you'd know she's never been a fan of me taking off. Being apart is pretty hard on us.

"But she has seen how much it has meant to me to have this opportunity."

Despite occasional appearances together on awards shows and festival stages, Chapman admitted that he didn't know many of his fellow Christian musicians before the *Young Messiah* tours.

"But it's to a point now—as Wayne Watson said at the close of one of the tours—where when we see a new album by one of the artists on this tour, or when we see them on a TV show, we view them in a whole different way. Now that person is a friend and you think back on specific things about them. This is one of your buddies who has experienced God's blessing!"

One of the odder pairings on the early tours was the immediate kinship between the outgoing, commanding Carman, and the shy, often self-effacing Chapman. The two hit it off immediately.

"Before that, I didn't know him at all," Chapman said. "But soon we got so close that one day we had a day off and Carman had an airline ticket for me—he really didn't give me a choice in the matter!—and said, `You're going to Tulsa with me. We're going to buy a Christmas tree.'

"I called my wife and said, `Honey, I could be going to Tulsa with Carman to pick out a Christmas tree on my day off instead of coming home. OK?' She said, `Go help Carman pick out a tree. He needs help!' So we went to Tulsa, hung out and really got to know each other."

The experience of spending time with artists like Carman, Wayne Watson, Bill and Gloria Gaither, Larnelle Harris and others led Chapman to write a song for his album *The Great Adventure* titled "Walk with the Wise."

"It's from Proverbs: `He who walks with the wise grows wise,'" Chapman said. "I think that's what *The Young Messiah* tours have been for me—time to walk with some *wise* guys.

"That first year I went out on the tour the Gaithers were on the show. Just sitting around the dinner table and hearing them tell stories, especially about their kids, was so amazing. Every time they'd talk about their family, they'd end up with tears in their eyes and you'd end up crying. I learned stuff from those conversations that I've put into use every day with my kids.

Tom Hemby's arrangement of "But Who May Abide the Day of His Coming?" turned the original vocal showcase into a moody, atmospheric ballad—perfect for Chapman's laid-back, acoustic style.

"The producers called and told me they wanted me to sing `But Who May Abide the Day of His Coming.' I must confess I was not familiar with the music of *Messiah*, other than hearing my brother perform it in choir in college.

"So I went and bought the original and listened to `But Who May Abide' and I thought `Hooo boy! This is going to be interesting!'

"But as I got into the process, put my heart into it, and worked to understand it, I immediately connected with what the lyric was saying."

And that lyric—as well as the other divinely inspired selections of Scripture that comprise *Messiah*—profoundly affected Chapman.

"Being involved in it and listening to it night after night, more

often than not I ended up in tears—even after hearing it so many times," he said. "By the power of the music, you sense that there is something going on beyond some talented guy opening the Bible and saying, `Oh! Let's try "But Who May Abide the Day of His Coming" and it goes a little something like this . . .'

"It was as if God breathed it and Handel wrote it down. It's that powerful."

With characteristic thoroughness, Chapman immediately immersed himself in Malachi and all of the prophetic texts of the Old Testament.

"I felt a sense of fear and trembling as I recorded it and as I sang it each night. I wanted to communicate to a large group of people—some of whom came just because it was Christmas music. I saw this as a great opportunity for the Holy Spirit to communicate the message of the Gospel to the people," he said. "So I really wanted to sing it passionately and understand what I was singing.

"The picture that came to me was of when I recently was out in the ocean deep sea fishing. A storm came up and the ocean got really rough. There was such incredible power that I quickly realized that I am a tiny speck in the grand scheme of things. One good wave could blow me over, I'd go down and never be heard from again. I felt a sense of fear.

"And yet this verse states that God is with us. This song prepares our minds to realize how bad off we are. It tells us just how bad the bad news is—so that the Good News becomes overwhelming.

"That's what I felt as I sang it night after night: when he appears, who could possibly stand in his presence? And yet, he cares for each of us. Amazing. Simply amazing."

> "It's from Proverbs: `He who walks with the wise grows wise', I think that's what *The Young Messiah* tours have been for me—time to walk with some *wise* guys."

Chapter 5

SUSAN ASHTON, CHRISTINE DENTÉ
AND CINDY MORGAN

"O Thou That Tellest Good Tidings to Zion"

Susan Ashton, Christine Denté, Cindy Morgan

O Zion, that bringest good tidings, get thee up into the high mountain; O Jerusalem, that bringest good tidings, lift up thy voice with strength; lift it up, be not afraid; say unto the cities of Judah, Behold your God! Arise, shine, for thy light is come, and the glory of the Lord is risen upon thee!

– Isaiah 40:9; 60:1

SUSAN ASHTON'S RECORDING CAREER began in 1991 with the Sparrow release of *Wakened by the Wind*. A year later, she released *Angels of Mercy*. In 1993, she was asked to sing on *The New Young Messiah*, *Songs from the Loft* and *Our Families* projects and record and

45

release her third album for Sparrow, *Susan Ashton*.

Oh yeah—she also got engaged in '93.

Not a bad year's work.

Asking her to name a favorite song or event from that year is like asking a parent to pick a favorite child. In front of the other children.

But there's no denying the excitement in Ashton's voice when she talks about recording "O Thou That Tellest Good Tidings to Zion" with Christine Denté and Cindy Morgan for *The New Young Messiah*.

T hat passion spills over into the performance itself. Over a gently swaying Latin-flavored beat, ace arranger Charlie Peacock crafts a sweet-spirited, reassuring lullaby, soothing enough to quiet even a frightened child. There is a momentary explosion of barely contained joy as the trio sings "Behold your God!", but the calming assurance quickly returns.

"I was excited to be asked to sing on *The New Young Messiah*, particularly with the trio," Ashton said. "I loved singing with Christine and Cindy.

"Someone thought it would be interesting to bring three young female artists together, not knowing how they'd blend. I think we were all pleasantly surprised with the results."

Interestingly, Ashton at first was not very familiar with *Messiah*.

"I'd heard it growing up, and especially remembered the The Hallelujah Chorus. But that was about it," she said. "So I was surprised and pleased when I was asked to be a part of it."

Since then Ashton has become a believer in Handel's immortal work.

"I think that it is great that they can take Messiah, such a traditional part of Christmas, and make it accessible to a whole new generation," she said. "I was interested in being part of something that communicates in a whole new way. I think it is a great accomplishment, one that I am proud to be part of."

"*The Young Messiah* is a concert that the whole family can enjoy," she said. "Christmas is about everybody's favorite time of the year. Something that can help us focus on the true meaning of Christmas and is enjoyable for the whole family—now *that's* a winner."

Few lyrics in the entire Bible are as poetic, as evocative, as powerful as the lines Ashton, Denté and Morgan sing in "O Thou That Tellest Good Tidings to Zion." Couple those with Handel's glorious music and Peacock's inspired arrangement and "O Thou That Tellest" becomes altogether transcendent.

"What this song does for me," Ashton said thoughtfully, "is this: When I sing it, it's as if I'm on top of a mountain proclaiming, `Everyone who thinks you don't have anything to live for. Everyone who thinks you can't get out of the hole you're in. You don't have to be sad or afraid! You can live! You do have something to live for! Someone is giving you life—brand new life, if you want it.'

"When we recorded the part that says, `Arise, shine, for thy light is come,' I remember the music hitting me. I felt like an eagle, soaring and free. I love that part of that song—what it says to me and what it says to the world."

As a result, Ashton says her involvement with *The Young Messiah* has become something she will always treasure.

"My hope is that *The Young Messiah* will communicate this message to all generations," she said.

"I hope that as families attend the concert and experience this together and listen to the record that it would keep this spiritual life fresh and new for them.

"Sometimes we can take our salvation for granted. Like a couple married thirty or forty years can take their relationship for granted. I hope *The Young Messiah* helps make our relationship with God fresh and new and alive."

Chapter **6**

BeBe & CeCe

"For Unto Us a Child Is Born"

BeBe & CeCe

For unto us a child is born, unto us a son is given, and the government shall be upon his shoulder; and his name shall be called Wonderful, Counseller, The mighty God, The everlasting Father, The Prince of Peace.

– Isaiah 9:6

YOUNG MESSIAH ARRANGER Cedric Caldwell has turned "For Unto Us a Child Is Born" into a church experience. And he's turned BeBe and CeCe Winans into revival preachers.

What begins as a silky, soulful mid-tempo ballad gradually becomes more and more insistent. BeBe's husky vocals alternate with CeCe's glorious soprano, then blend as only sibling harmonies can. The music, propelled by the deep-bottomed rhythm section, slowly, subtly increases in intensity. BeBe and CeCe are more emphatic now—the birth of the Savior must be told, it must be shared.

And, by the close, both artists are testifying the Good News, caught up in the rapture and lost in the joy of the moment.

It is one of the transcendent moments in *The Young Messiah*. And it is yet another reminder of why BeBe and CeCe have enjoyed spectacular success in both mainstream and Christian music worlds.

"For Unto Us a Child Is Born" has a rich and varied history even apart from Handel's epic *Messiah*. It is largely comprised of re-worked material from the first movement of one of Handel's earlier Italian opera-styled duets.

In the movements that precede "For Unto Us a Child Is Born," Handel has tempered the announcement that "Behold a virgin shall conceive" with a stark reminder that indeed "darkness shall cover the earth" in the days before the coming of the long-promised Messiah.

As for the lyrics, what is left to be said about the Child whose birth is considered by even non-Christians as the center point of history? All events are explained as being either before or after his birth. It is among the most important events in history, spoken in the same breath with Christ's death and Resurrection.

B ut what do we know of the Child called *Wonderful, Counseller, The mighty God, The everlasting Father, The Prince of Peace?* Very little really. It probably wasn't cold that day he was born, and it almost certainly wasn't December 25th.

His parents were nobodies, part of the great crowds of peoples dispossessed by the vagaries of Roman law. His mother wasn't even married when he was born in the humble cave in Bethlehem. And yet, the vicious Herod so feared this tiny Babe that he had his armies murder a generation of male children in the City of David. And, an unknown number of astrologer kings—the Magi—thought it important enough to travel across a hostile continent to pay homage to him.

Just a few miles away in Jerusalem, the leaders of a nation that had prayed for this Messiah for two thousand years didn't hear a word or see a thing. And yet a handful of ragged, illiterate shepherds were dazzled with one of the most awesome celestial displays in recorded history, a dance of enraptured, ecstatic angels, rejoicing in the sky over the birth of the Son of God.

Generally, the Biblical narrative does not dwell on kings and armies, but on individuals—as befitting a Messiah who someday would choose a donkey over a white charger to enter Jerusalem.

After hearing Mary's amazing story of the angel's announcement that she would give birth to the Messiah, Elizabeth cries, "You are favored by God above all other women, and your child is destined for God's mightiest praise! What an honor this is, that the mother of my Lord should visit me!" The child that will become John the Baptist leaps in Elizabeth's womb in the presence of the Messiah to come. The priest Zechariah ends nine months of silence with an explosive hymn of praise. Ancient Simeon, who God promised would not die until he had seen the Messiah, instinctively

Handel may have had a reason for placing "For Unto Us" between two more reflective, even somber pieces. Maybe he is reminding us that while it is appropriate to celebrate the birth of the Child, the birth is only a step on the road to the Cross and the Resurrection that follows.

knows his long wait is at an end. And the prophetess Anna, who had remained steadfastly in the temple, praying ceaselessly, knows her work is almost done.

And then after his birth this blessed Child disappears from the Scripture except for a curious event where he leaves his parents to return to the temple to lecture the lecturers.

The next time he appears, it is as a young man about to embark on a three-year journey that will lead to a hideous death at the hands of a Roman torture machine.

And on that day, the day of his crucifixion, at his bloody feet stands his mother Mary—his lone link to that mystical, magical night in Bethlehem.

What must Mary have thought as she watched his precious life's blood drip away? Did she remember her spontaneous Magnificat (Luke 1:46-55)? Did she recall the thousand and one images of his childhood, images none of us will know until we meet him face to face?

> *By the close, both artists are testifying the Good News, caught up in the rapture and lost in the joy of the moment.*

Seeing him die, did she suddenly doubt—remembering the promises the angelic host made for her Babe? They sang that he would be called Wonderful, Counsellor, The mighty God, The everlasting Father, The Prince of Peace.

And what about the part of "the government (being) upon his shoulders"? All she could see on her Son's shoulders this day were the strips of torn flesh from the Roman scourge.

Or did Mary alone know that the Crucifixion was only the beginning? Did she hide his words in her heart and retire to pray in the three days following his death?

Probably not.

Despite three years of intensive preaching, senses-shattering miracles and a life lived in unparalleled holiness, the Bible records not a single person who knew beyond a shadow of a doubt that after the Crucifixion would come the Resurrection.

What is the message here? Handel may have had a reason for placing "For Unto Us" between two more reflective, even somber pieces. Maybe he is reminding us that while it is appropriate to celebrate the birth of the Child, the birth is only a step on the road to the Cross and the Resurrection that follows.

In Handel's time Messiah was performed more regularly at Easter than at Christmas.

Perhaps it should be at Easter—not Christmas—that we celebrate with gifts and merrymaking. Perhaps the Resurrection   the one event that separates this faith from all the world's religions— should be our focal point, not Christmas. Perhaps we should concentrate more on the empty tomb than the Judean manger.

In fact, in Handel's time—and in the centuries that followed—*Messiah* was performed more regularly at Easter than at Christmas. Only in the latter part of this century has it become identified with Christmas.

Ultimately, of course, it doesn't matter *when* this *Messiah* is performed, but *why*. It matters not how it is performed, but how its message impacts those who hear it.

"Let him who has ears to hear . . ."

Handel's last public appearance was on Good Friday, 1759—at a performance of *Messiah*. At its conclusion, he collapsed. He died that glorious Easter weekend.

The great man had earned his rest.

Chapter 7

PHIL KEAGGY

"PASTORALE"

Phil Keaggy

OF ALL THE MULTI-COLORED THREADS that make up the tapestry of Handel's *Messiah,* the "Pastorale" adds the beauty of muted, burnished gold. In *Messiah,* Handel adroitly uses the "Pastorale" to set the mood for the shepherd's scene that follows, "He Shall Feed His Flock."

As the narrative of *The Young Messiah* approaches the Christmas story, using a few solo strings and a soothing rhythm, arranger/orchestrator Blair Masters suddenly has the chorus break into a short, staccato chant, only to return to the idyllic guitar once again.

On the recorded version of *The Young Messiah*, that guitar part is played by Phil Keaggy.

Keaggy is, of course, the first choice for virtually any guitar part. For more than two decades, the slim, shy virtuoso has dazzled the instrumental world with his musicianship. He's also recorded a host of critically acclaimed and commercially successful albums for the contemporary Christian marketplace.

Even in the short time allotted to him in "Pastorale," Keaggy's warm, precise style is immediately recognizable.

"The producers of *The Young Messiah* have attempted to introduce people to *Messiah* and give them a greater appreciation for an incredible work of art," Keaggy said. "It is not only a work of art, it is also a spiritual event. And modern ears are more attuned to the sounds of contemporary and pop music. So what they've done with *The Young Messiah* is bring this message to a contemporary audience.

Keaggy says his participation in *The Young Messiah* has made an impact on his musical outlook—perhaps more than any other artist involved with the project.

"I've grown to appreciate Handel's message even more through it," he said. "I was on the first *Young Messiah* tour where every night I heard the orchestra, the voices, the melody and the emotion that was written into it. Handel has his own extraordinary style, just as all composers do.

"I grew so intrigued by *Messiah*, I purchased and became familiar with more of Handel's music. And I think it all is brilliant."

But heavenly melodies alone do not guarantee musical immortality. Keaggy says the key to *Messiah's* longevity has as much to do with the lyric content as the sublime music.

"*Messiah* has endured because at its center is the picture painted in Isaiah 53 of the Promised One coming, suffering, rising from the dead," Keaggy said, "and because it conveys the majesty of Jesus the Messiah. It touches something in the hearts of all people—a longing for his return.

"I think Handel struck a chord in his audiences with *Messiah*. And I understand this was a momentous experience for Handel. In the process of creating this piece, he was personally met by God."

If a work is inspired by God, Keaggy reasons, then no amount of musical modernization will diminish its divinely ordained power.

It's not surprising that Keaggy is sympathetic to that supposition. His career spans the breadth of contemporary Christian music, from the early hardscrabble days of Jesus Music to recent award-winning releases like *Way Back Home, Crimson & Blue* and the instrumental *The Wind and the Wheat.*

Keaggy has effortlessly, seamlessly remained both musically current and lyrically relevant.

"If the update is done in the right spirit, if the producers have the right reasons, and if the artists involved have a real heart for it, then contemporizing *Messiah* can reach even more people with its message," Keaggy said.

"That doesn't mean I would throw away my King James Bible just because I have a modern translation. The old and new complement each other.

"In the same way, God uses this recording and this production to continually win hearts around the world."

As for his part in *The Young Messiah,* "Pastorale," Keaggy is typically self-effacing. "I don't read music, so I had to repeatedly listen to the melody—which is pretty complicated, it turns around and about in different ways—before I could play it. I think what they wanted was a sense of "real fingers" to draw out the melody from the beautiful orchestra tions. That was my contribution.

"I think it is a lovely section of the album, though, and I'm really glad that I'm identified with it."

In the end, Keaggy compares *The Young Messiah* with the popular film *Jesus.* "The film has made the gospel story understandable in different languages all over the world," he said. "It is a tremendous tool of evangelism. I think The Young Messiah also is evangelistic in the most respected and reverent form.

"It is a celebration as well, as all of the voices, hearts and minds of people join to celebrate this event.

"When it is performed, it is a little bit of heaven on earth, a small sample of what will come in the Kingdom of Heaven when we all lay our crowns before God. I just can't wait to lay my crown before him!"

Chapter 8

CARMAN

"GLORY TO GOD IN THE HIGHEST"

Carman

Glory to God in the highest, and on earth, peace, good will toward men.

– Luke 2:14

CARMAN—NO LAST NAME USED or needed—is something else. His albums and long-play videos like *The Standard, Addicted to Jesus* and *Revival in the Land* have gone gold and platinum. He packs 20,000-seat arenas—yet generally won't charge for tickets. Though it's hard to define his musical style, he has carved a giant niche for himself as a singer, musician, storyteller and performer.

He is that rare artist—Christian or otherwise—with a larger-than-life persona, a personal charisma and a clear-eyed, clearly expressed faith and direction.

"On earlier tours, I sang `The Trumpet Shall Sound,'" he recalled from his Tulsa, Oklahoma, office, "It was the most difficult thing I'd ever done! I sweated through it every time."

He also served as co-host of the show, but admitted that the adjustment from headlining his own tours to becoming a cast member on *The Young Messiah* was difficult at first.

"I had to adjust to not being responsible for an entire tour," he said. "At first I would walk in and automatically say, `We need to fix this' and `What happened here?' and `These people need to come in here.' It was instinctive from years of being in charge on my tours.

"So it took me a few concerts to get used to not having anything to worry about but singing. But once I got used to it, I *really* got used to it!"

Carman, like all of the other artists, also enjoyed the inevitable "hanging" with other artists.

"That's the cool part, the thing I enjoy the most," he said. "It's really relaxing."

Well, not *completely* relaxing. After a few nights on the tour, as artists' friendships grew, the inevitable teasing and practical joking began. Often at the source, Carman said, was BeBe Winans.

For instance, most of the artists tried not to duplicate anything others said. After a few shows, there was an unspoken agreement that Steven Curtis Chapman would say "Merry Christmas, everybody!" at the close of the first half.

"But BeBe would get up and say `Merry Christmas' *before* Steven Curtis," Carman recalled with a chuckle. "So that way when Steven Curtis said it, it sounded like he was copying BeBe.

"Then, after a few more shows, I got up and I said it before BeBe, so it looked like he was copying me!"

But even Winans had to admit that Carman's rendition of "Glory to God in the Highest" is a showstopping original. Carman receives an immediate reaction from the audience, turning the song into a funky interactive praise and worship chorus. He is part street evangelist, part rapper, part narrator. And by the end of the song, everyone knows the difference between *announcement* and *pronouncement*!

"In `Glory to God,' you can see the way I instinctively approach a song," he said. "I'm there to minister. I believe music was created by God for us to worship him with. Even though music has many forms, the greatest expression is in praise and worship to the Lord. What I aim to do to the best of my ability is follow God's plan for music and use it to invite people to worship.

But as fun and bouncy as is the urban gospel of `Glory to God in the Highest' (arranged and programmed by Robbie Buchanan), to Carman the music is only the vehicle to spread the Message contained in the lyric:

"The Scripture says,

> *And suddenly there was with the angel a multitude of the heavenly host praising God, and saying, Glory to God in the highest, and on earth peace, good will toward men.* (Luke 2:13–14)

The important thing is that this message came to the shepherds.

"The Scripture goes on to say,

> *And it came to pass, as the angels were gone away from them into heaven, the shepherds said one to another, Let us now go even unto Bethlehem, and see this thing which is come to pass, which the Lord hath made known unto us. And they came with haste, and found Mary and Joseph, and the babe lying in a manger. And when they had seen it, they made known abroad the saying which was told them concerning this child. And all they that heard it wondered at those things which were told them by the shepherds.* (Luke 2:15–18)

Carman says that the shepherds represent to him the pastors of the modern Church.

"Pastors are the ones who oversee the flocks," he said. "God reveals his directives corporately to the shepherds who then preach them to the people.

"So to me this Scripture deals with the authority God has given the local church pastors. As in New Testament times, it is the same today: God is ministering to the shepherds and the shepherds take what they have seen and heard and preach it to the people.

"I believe this is an encouragement to lock into your local church and to be committed and to listen to what your pastor has to say."

And like the other artists, Carman looks forward to participating in The Hallelujah Chorus each performance.

"The word itself, *hallelujah*, means `a song of praise to Jehovah,'" he said. "*Hallel* literally means `jump around and be foolish clamorously.' *Ujah* is the unpronounceable name of God with some vowels in it. It actually means `to be clamorously foolish unto the Lord.' So the word itself describes praise and worship.

"The Bible says, `God inhabits the praise of his people.' As people sing that word over and over and become more demonstrative with it, the presence of the Lord fills that auditorium. And people respond to it like it is the first time they ever heard it—because the presence of the Lord never gets old. It's refreshing every time.

"It becomes a worship chorus; people begin to worship the Lord. As we begin to sing `Hallelujah' and offer this praise to Jehovah, God makes himself present and begins to minister life to people."

"And this is the real thing. Believer or non-believer alike—all are affected by the presence of the Lord."

Chapter *9*

FIRST CALL

"REJOICE GREATLY, O DAUGHTER OF ZION"

First Call

Rejoice greatly, O daughter of Zion; shout, O daughter of Jerusalem; behold, thy King cometh unto thee; he is just, and having salvation . . . He shall speak peace unto the heathen.

– Zechariah 9:9–10

THERE ARE FEW MOMENTS in *The Young Messiah* that can match the sheer joy of First Call's "Rejoice Greatly, O Daughter of Zion." It is a rapid-fire a cappella triumph. An angel chorus singing doo-wop harmonies. The Manhattan Transfer goes baroque. It is a giddy, joyous moment that only First Call could pull off.

Since 1985, First Call mainstays Marty McCall and Bonnie Keen have been just about everywhere and done everything in contemporary Christian music. Their close harmonies have graced a thousand recording sessions even as their own albums have topped the charts and earned the group a dozen Dove nominations.

"This album contains some amazing moments for me," Bonnie Keen recalled. "I still listen to it a lot. Greg Nelson's production and the different arrangers they brought in really meshed together. I think what resulted is amazing."

> "I think this song is the perfect marriage of lyric and music, conveying that feeling of rejoicing greatly—for the King really is coming!"

Most of the artists on *The Young Messiah* recording were able to join the '93 tour—including, for the first time, First Call.

"We'd heard a lot about *The Young Messiah* being a spectacular night of music," Keen said. "But I'd never seen it so I didn't quite know what to expect.

"It was glorious. The music is excellent. It was inspiring to see the caliber of talent on that stage. Hearing all the different styles gave me a new perspective that you don't get in your own little corner, singing your own style of music.

"*The Young Messiah* is something I'm proud to be part of. It was not only inspiring, but fun."

Keen said during the tour she had as much fun off/stage as on.

"We had around twenty artists on the bus together. Usually, we only see each other once a year at the Gospel Music Association meeting, or we'll see some of them in the studio," she said.

"But it was incredible to be around the other artists for longer periods of time.

"We had devotions every night where we shared what was going on in our lives. My favorite part of the tour was offstage, being around those other artists and getting to know them better."

Keen had vivid memories of other backstage moments on *The*

Young Messiah as well: talks with conductor Ralph Carmichael, prayers with Steve Green, intimate chats with CeCe Winans and devotionals by Larnelle Harris.

"Larnelle delivered some powerful devotionals on the tour," she said. "At the end, we'd all be bawling because of the intimate, deep wells of faith he shared—about wrestling with God, about walking his walk.

"I think the audiences picked up on the camaraderie among the singers and musicians—we became one big loving family during the tour. It is one of the few times we meet on this musical common ground."

Another highlight for Keen was the appearance each night of a different local choir, usually drawn from area church choirs.

"They would work on this for weeks," she said. "And they were so excited. It was fun to see choir members from the different cities around the country become energized by the performances. I enjoyed watching them as they experienced the entire evening."

Incidentally, more than one critic used the word *amazing* to describe First Call's tongue-twisting rendition of "Rejoice Greatly, O Daughter of Zion." Keen admitted that because of the nature of the music she didn't have much time to reflect on the lyrics—until later.

"Rejoice Greatly' is all a cappella and it was extremely difficult," she said. "We pushed long and hard to master it. It was a pleasure to sing, but the execution was such that it wasn't until later that I could listen to what we were saying.

"And what I heard then was powerful, especially when you think of the time it was written. It speaks to me of rejoicing in the midst of turmoil and chaos. It speaks directly to me of faith.

"I think this song is the perfect marriage of lyric and music, conveying that feeling of rejoicing greatly—for the King really is coming!"

Keen considers "Rejoice Greatly" one of First Call's finest moments on tape—ever.

"Besides the arrangement and the support, part of that is due to its straightforward, impassioned lyric," she said. "I'm glad that while it is so powerful lyrically it is extremely clear in its message. "

During the live performance of *The Young Messiah*, Keen also joins Sandi Patty and former First Call member Marabeth Jordan singing the background vocals on "Lift Up Your Heads, O Ye Gates."

"That was my favorite part of the night," Keen said, "because it isn't as complicated or demanding as `Rejoice Greatly' and I could relax a little.

"And it is also then that I can really get a sense of the audience. They see us interacting and it makes this song a joy for them as well.

"But `Rejoice Greatly' is one of those vocally spectacular moments where we just held on for the ride. If we had stopped, we would have really gotten lost. Thankfully, that never happened, but it took a lot of focus for all three of us to pull it off."

But no matter the complexity of her particular song or songs, Keen said there is no real mystery to *Messiah's* three-century success. She says it can be boiled down to two factors: music and lyrics.

"People are drawn to beautiful melodies," she said. "Messiah is timeless. It has some of the most beautiful melodies ever written.

"Secondly, lyrics like `Comfort Ye My People,' `Lift Up Your Heads, O Ye Gates,' `Rejoice Greatly O Daughter of Zion' and the others focus on themes that appeal to people. These are strong sentiments pulled straight out of the Scripture that people can live by. Like the melodies, they're timeless. Look how these songs have transcended the years. Great songs do that. They'll draw people in any age group."

Keen calls it "miraculous" how the Holy Spirit worked through Handel.

"It is a miracle," she said, "how God transcends souls and eras. And this piece of music does that on every level, every time."

Does Keen have a favorite song or passage in the work? It's no surprise that there is one piece of music that moves her like no other: "The Hallelujah Chorus. It is simply unbelievable. The arrangement we use on the record and on the tour is my favorite arrangement ever. It is so exciting to be in an arena with fifteen thousand people, feeling momentum building, listening to Larnelle and Sandi and CeCe cut loose, and watching those two incredible dancers. It is a culmination of the evening's performance, simply because it is so celebratory.

"The end result is a life-changing moment, where the music and the lyrics take on a life of their own."

> *"These are strong sentiments pulled straight out of the Scripture that people can live by. Like the melodies, they're timeless.*"

Before the 1993 tour began, producer Greg Nelson and conductor Ralph Carmichael told BeBe and CeCe Winans to "cut loose" during the final bars of The Hallelujah Chorus, to improvise as the Spirit moves them.

"That took the `Chorus' to a whole different level," Keen said, still slightly in awe. "CeCe stood right in front of me. And she's so humble, not a show-off at all, but these amazing notes would burst forth from her night after night.

"God's hand certainly was in this *Young Messiah*."

Keen paused a moment, lost in thought.

"Maybe God's hand is in every *Messiah*."

Chapter 10

STEVEN CURTIS CHAPMAN
AND SANDI PATTY

"HE SHALL FEED HIS FLOCK"

Steven Curtis Chapman and Sandi Patty

He shall feed his flock like a shepherd; and he shall gather the lambs with his arm, and carry them in his bosom, and shall gently lead those that are with young.

– Isaiah 40:11

THESE DAYS, YOU CAN HARDLY escape seeing—or hearing—Steven Curtis Chapman. His boyish grin adorns shelves in bookstores and smiles placidly from magazine jackets. His latest release, *Heaven in the Real World*, debuted at #1 on *Billboard* magazine's charts. His songs fill the airwaves. And in the summer of 1994, he embarked on a record-breaking seventy-city U.S. tour, followed by an unprecedented world tour.

Since 1987, his seven albums have produced a host of #1 singles, sold several million units, earned him three Grammy Awards, and a couple dozen Dove Awards. He's appeared on national television shows, written songs for the likes of Billy Dean and Charlie Daniels, and is one of the most popular artists around.

And something else—he's also remained a nice guy who is devoted to his family.

One thing Chapman is excited to talk about is a duet he recorded with Sandi Patty for *The Young Messiah,* a moving version of "He Shall Feed His Flock."

Both artists came out of the experience complimenting the other.

"When it came time to sing with Sandi, I was afraid it was going to be very intimidating," Chapman said with a stricken look on his face.

"But it was a real treat and a thrill for me. This is the comment that most of my friends and family made after seeing the show: `A duet with Sandi Patty! I guess that means you've arrived.'"

"One of the most enjoyable things about the *Young Messiah* tour was singing each night with Steven," Patty adds. "He truly has a humble, sensitive spirit. He's really like what he appears on stage—except he's funnier off-stage."

As arranged by Robbie Buchanan, "He Shall Feed His Flock" is one of the more traditional songs in *The Young Messiah.* Stately, lyrical, it begins with the two solos, then culminates with the duet between Chapman and Patty. It's a unique combination of voices, with the harmonies blending nicely creating a comforting and illuminating effect.

Patty said that as she sang "He Shall Feed His Flock" it felt like a part of her own life journey.

"That song is so tender," she said. "It helps us see Jesus as the Good Shepherd who takes care of the one that's lost."

"He Shall Feed His Flock" was equally emotional for Chapman.

"Every night I sang that song to the dad who was there because Mom and the kids dragged him along," he said. "Or to the couple who really has no idea what Christmas is all about, but was invited by their next-door neighbors who said, `C'mon! It's a Christmas program.'

"So every night I tried to imagine the guy sitting there with the weight of the world on his shoulders, thinking of the bills stacking up because of the holidays—who has lost the true meaning of Christmas. I focused on those people out there who carried an incredibly heavy load."

In those words from Isaiah, Chapman said he hears the echoes of the Christ-to-come, the Jesus who will reach out to souls just like that distracted man or that unbelieving couple in the audience.

"For me, in this lyric Jesus is saying, `Take my yoke upon you and I will give you rest for your soul,'" Chapman said. "And that's important. In light of that hopelessness that's laying like a ton of bricks on the hearts of people—it's amazing to stand there and sing that message that Christ pleads with us to put down this heavy weight that we were never intended to carry. And if we do, we find rest for our souls."

And in those few lines of Scripture, Chapman believes, are the crux of our faith.

"It's a paradox and deeply profound. Yet it's also amazingly simple. Only the Scripture can be so profoundly simple," he said, shaking his head in wonder.

"It was my prayer when I sang 'He Shall Feed His Flock' every night that it would be for the people in the audience a time that the Spirit could move in their hearts saying, `Hey, wouldn't you like to find rest for your soul? Can you imagine that? It really exists. Just listen . . .'

"It's a powerful message to proclaim."

But then, it was always meant to be.

Chapter 11

LARNELLE HARRIS, STEVE GREEN
AND MICHAEL ENGLISH

"Surely He Hath Borne Our Griefs"

Larnelle Harris, Steve Green, Michael English

Surely he hath borne our griefs and carried our sorrows . . .
He was wounded for our transgressions, he was bruised for
our iniquities; the chastisement of our peace was upon him.

– Isaiah 53:4–5

IN *THE YOUNG MESSIAH*, arranger Alan Moore has turned "Surely He Hath Borne Our Griefs" into a sweetly sorrowful lament for three voices. He's scored it at the top of the register for tenors and baritones alike and crafted it into a haunting ballad filled with expressions of exquisite pain and longing.

   "When I read or sing this passage, I cry—I have tears right now," Larnelle Harris said. "We spend so much time glorifying the Crucifixion, dwelling on the nailprints in Jesus' hands, that it almost becomes a ditty.

We must *never* let that happen. What we're doing is describing the most awful, most painful, most cruel way to die that any human has ever inflicted on another.

"And yet, Jesus could have called legions of angels to defend himself. Or he could have shouted, `Enough!' Instead, he gave up a kingdom to come here, to suffer all of this, and thought nothing about it—so I could have life.

"If I had to give up my firstborn son to save your life, you'd be in bad shape. I couldn't do it. But that's what God did for you and me. And in doing so, he claimed victory over the grave so we could live again. He didn't have to do that for us!

"And if that doesn't bring tears to your eyes . . . "

"Surely He Hath Borne Our Griefs" is one of the mystical moments in *The Young Messiah*. It is understated, not somber or dirge-like but without the dramatic ending of some of the other songs. And Harris likes it that way.

"It simply states through a haunting melody and lyrics the thesis of that precious verse," he said. "In it, Jesus cries, `Look at my tears, look at the blood I shed. I did it all for you.'

"Of all of the incredible songs in *Messiah*, this one alone was written with the sinner in mind. If after hearing that lyric you *still* don't understand God's love for us, then you're not going to understand. As Bill Gaither says, `If you can't build a fire with that, then your wood's wet.'"

Singing with that level of conviction, that level of passion night after night can be draining—both emotionally and spiritually—but it is a price that Harris is willing to pay.

"I don't ever want to lose that intense feeling," he said. "Sure, I have nights when I am tired and it is difficult to be up there singing. But there's always something in *The Young Messiah* for me. Sometimes when I lack strength, my 'youth is renewed like eagles.' Something in that performance gets to me—no matter how many times I've heard it before. There's something every night—usually it is this very song—that ministers to me."

But how has *Messiah* not only survived over the past 250 years, but actually grown in stature and popularity?

"I believe it has endured and prospered because it is scriptural," Harris said. "Many people don't know that Handel was a Christian whose great compassion and generosity caused him to give most of the *Messiah* performance proceeds away. He wrote the entire oratorio as it was dictated to him from above, out of his love for people, and out of his love for Someone much higher than himself. When something is developed in love, it shows itself by a spirit of giving rather than a spirit of, `Listen to this great composition that just came out of my mind!'

"So hundreds of years later people still come to hear *Messiah*. It continues to catch the attention year after year of both Christian and mainstream communities."

> "If I had to give up my firstborn son to save your life, you'd be in bad shape. I couldn't do it. But that's what God did for you and me."

In Harris's twenty-five years of musical ministry, he's become a keen observer of his audiences and of the human condition in general. When he says that *The Young Messiah* compels the attention of saved and unsaved alike, it is a statement based on years of observation, on decades of interacting with untold thousands of listeners.

"I can tell if the *Young Messiah* audience is drawn primarily from the church or from across the community by their responses in various places," he said. "In church-dominated audiences, there is thunderous applause at the end of certain dramatic anthems. But other audiences are not always comfortable there. We need always be aware of everybody out there, not just the churchgoers. We don't want this to be for the insider only, we want it to be something everyone can enjoy."

> "Rather than audiences going out humming `Jingle Bells', we hope that everyone leaves knowing that the Lord was here."

Messiah, Harris believes, gives audiences that seasonal music they're craving, but it also gives them something more.

"We're talking about the Messiah, how he bore my griefs and my sorrow," Harris said. "And, at the end of the evening, we offer an opportunity to raise your hands, clap and stomp your feet and worship any way you like.

"Rather than audiences going out humming `Jingle Bells', we hope that everyone leaves knowing that the Lord was here. This Christ, who was born of a virgin, died and was raised, is here, waiting to be in their hearts. And, hopefully, they will acknowledge his presence in their lives."

Ultimately, Harris maintains that this kind of inspiration and impact must be divine. It is divine inspiration alone that can reach through time and remain as relevant and moving today as in Handel's day.

"I think that's what brings people back year after year," Harris said. "People feel something, and that something is God. Then when they leave they can say, `Now I'm ready for Christmas!'

"And that's because—`surely he hath borne our griefs'—the work is done! The hard part is over. All that's left is to claim the victory!"

Chapter *12*

STEVE GREEN

"I Know That My Redeemer Liveth"

Steve Green

I know that my redeemer liveth, and that he shall stand at the latter day upon the earth: And though . . . worms destroy this body, yet in my flesh shall I see God.

– Job 19:25–26

WHEN YOU TRAVEL TOGETHER in close quarters for a month or more, the last thing you want to do is hurt one of your fellow traveler's feelings. So when most of the artists on *The Young Messiah* are asked if they have a favorite moment or song during the performance, virtually all politely decline to name just one.

But if you press them, a number of the artists privately admit—off the record, of course—that Steve Green's stunning performance of "I Know That My Redeemer Liveth" moves them to tears nearly every time they hear it.

And with good reason. It is an utterly believable, triumphant moment. Green sings with fervor and clear-eyed conviction in a strong, compelling voice. And when he allows himself a smile on the word *liveth*, the joy in his face is transparent.

Of course, Green's life and works must be factored into the equation. Coming from an artist who has made evangelism and personal holiness lifelong commitments, "I Know That My Redeemer Liveth" carries an additional emotional wallop.

In the past decade, Green has won virtually every award gospel music has to offer. Songs like "People Need the Lord," "He Holds the Keys," "Find Us Faithful" and "The Mission" have moved from the radio airwaves into the churches. And amid it all he's continued his missionary parents' work by traveling far and wide on behalf of the Body of Christ.

So when you ask Steve Green a question, expect a serious, thoughtful answer:

"Someone asked me during this past tour, `What do you think about while you sing this song?'

"I said, `I'm thinking about all of the implications of the Resurrection, that in Christ's death, we died with him, but in the Resurrection we are raised with him. And we are raised to walk in a newness of life. And because of the Resurrection, we have been delivered from the power of sin so that we no longer have to continue a life of disobedience and shame, but we are set free to become servants of righteousness.'"

Whoa! Now *that's* a typical Steve Green answer!

Green said he first heard *Messiah* when his college choir sang it.

"I remember it well," he said. It was one of the high points of my college choir experience. I still remember the sections working through all of the parts, especially the glorious tenor parts—and all of us young tenors stretching our necks to reach those high passages!"

Since then, Green said he's come to regard *Messiah* not only as one of the most creative oratorios ever written, but as a priceless, life-changing evangelical tool.

"Because it has been tied to Christmas, it has more enduring historical strength," he said. "But it also has survived because the music is soul-stirring and recognizable.

"Maybe most importantly, *Messiah* has flourished because it is Scripture. God blesses this musical composition, because this is his Word. The Word of God penetrates hearts, powerfully impacting people's lives.

"The Resurrection is the crux of Christianity It defeated death, proved the deity of Christ and gave us hope of everlasting life. And the theme of the Resurrection flows all through the Scriptures—and *Messiah*."

But Green believes the performances and recordings of *The Young Messiah* have had additional sometimes unexpected benefits beyond evangelism, particularly to the cast and crew.

"Some of my best memories are of the friendships that have developed on the tour," he said. "We all tour and record, each with our own different style and philosophy.

"But *The Young Messiah* tour is a time for us to break down barriers and recognize our common calling. It has become a valuable bonding

> "*Messiah* has flourished because it is Scripture. God blesses this musical composition, because this is his Word. The Word of God penetrates hearts, powerfully impacting people's lives."

time for me, particularly with some of the guys."

That bonding forged in nightly prayer sessions and Bible studies, as well as the camaraderie that develops on long bus trips has created a stronger, more unified *Young Messiah* cast. Green believes that unity lends credence to what they sing about.

After all, if there isn't harmony on the stage by artists telling the greatest story ever told, how can they expect that story to change the lives of those listening?

"The whole package—the great arrangements, the heart-tugging melodies and the powerful lyrics—is a moving experience," Green said. "And yet it crosses my mind even as I sing this powerful song that nothing happens unless we grasp by faith the truth and it becomes embedded in our hearts. It is easy to be stirred emotionally but to remain helplessly crippled because we haven't appropriated that truth.

"So, when I sing `I Know That My Redeemer Liveth,' two things come to mind: One is the triumph of this lyric of Christ's Resurrection and the other is the sorrow in my own heart that so many don't accept it."

Green sees every performance as an opportunity to share the Good News.

"Every night of *The Young Messiah* I'll see people in the audience who seem unfamiliar with the Message," Green said. "Some may have come out of curiosity, some because it is a seasonal extravaganza. But I hope and trust that they don't get caught up in the glitter, the pizzazz of singers and the songs and miss the heart of it, the substance of the Gospel.

"We singers are dependent on God to change them. Because no one has ever been changed by a song. It's God who does the changing."

For the first time during the interview, Green laughs.

"So we're really pretty helpless up there!" he adds modestly. "Only God can open their hearts to understand."

Chapter 13

MICHAEL ENGLISH

"LIFT UP YOUR HEADS, O YE GATES"

Michael English

Lift up your heads, O ye gates; and be ye lift up, ye ever-lasting doors; and the King of glory shall come in. Who is the King of glory? The Lord strong and mighty, the Lord mighty in battle. Lift up your heads, O ye gates; even lift them up, ye everlasting doors; and the King of glory shall come in.

– Psalms 24:7-9

THE SCENE WAS THE BEAUTIFUL new Pantheon in London, the most glorious, the most ornate hall England had ever seen. The event, held in May 1784, was the centennial of Handel's birth. All of London's elite were there—including George III and his Queen, royal patrons of the first "Handel Commemoration." The triumphant notes of Messiah rang through London.

As the performance ended the impact was so profound that the Queen commanded the entire work be performed again—immediately!

And during the second performance of "Lift Up Your Heads, O Ye Gates," when the full chorus and orchestra began the resounding "He Is the King of Glory," the entire audience—and all of the performers—spontaneously burst into tears of joy.

As one historian notes, "Perhaps the subjects of no sovereign prince on the globe were ever before so delighted with the effects of a royal mandate."

"Lift Up Your Heads, O Ye Gates" is intriguing among the passages of Messiah for other reasons. For instance, it contains Handel's only five-part writing in Messiah.

And, just as he resisted the obvious tactic of setting the somber, melancholy "He Was Despised" in a minor key, Handel resisted the temptation to trivialize the Ascension with showy flourishes and a bombastic full orchestral treatment, preferring instead a majestically simple approach, letting the words speak for themselves.

"Who is the King of Glory"? the song asks on two different occasions. Until we know the answer to that question, we'll never open the gates of our hearts. Until we acknowledge the Lord of Hosts, we'll never let him in.

Musically, "Lift Up Your Heads" consists of a question-and-answer format—a stylistic device still used today in Gospel music, but known as "call-and-response." And that is how arranger Robbie Buchanan chose to interpret the piece for The Young Messiah, complete with rollicking beat and room for vocal improvisations at the end.

Lyrically, though, "Lift Up Your Heads, O Ye Gates" may seem a little vague to modern-day readers. Gates aren't generally considered to have "heads"—and why is the Psalmist asking *them* questions about the identity of the King of Glory?

But to those living in Biblical times, the allusion was perfectly clear. Most major cities were walled for defensive purposes, with the gates being the only way in and out. Jerusalem's gates even had popular, familiar names. And in times of crisis, the gates were closed and barred.

The word *gate* can also mean "power" in the Bible. God tells Abraham, "Thy seed shall possess the *gate* of his enemies" (Gen. 22:17). And Christ proclaims, "And I say also unto thee, That thou art Peter, and upon this rock I will build my church; and the *gates* of hell shall not prevail against it" (Matt. 16:18).

But probably the more familiar use of *gate* in Scripture is to describe *access*. The City of God is said to have twelve gates: "And the city had no need of the sun, neither of the moon, to shine in it: for the glory of God did lighten it, and the Lamb is the light thereof. And the nations of them which are saved shall walk in the light of it: and the kings of the earth do bring their glory and honour unto it. And the gates of it shall not be shut at all by day: for there shall be no night there." (Rev. 21:23–25).

"Its gates shall never be shut"—that must have been comforting to the poor, battered Hebrews who periodically were overrun by Egyptian, Babylonian, Assyrian and Roman alike.

It's a comfort to people of all ages as well. The gate to the holy city—which is the Message of salvation in Jesus Christ—will never be closed. As the parable of the laborers in the vineyard (Matt. 20) makes plain, those arriving late will be rewarded just as surely as those who arrive early.

It's a funny thing about gates, though. Because they generally are for defense, they are meant to be opened from the inside. People standing outside the gate must wait until someone inside allows them in. The familiar painting of Christ standing outside the door with no doorknob is

a good example. The Message— the Risen Christ—is standing outside our door, our gate. But only we inside can let Him in.

An ancient Advent hymn says it well:

> Lift up your heads, ye mighty gates,
> Behold, the King of Glory waits;
> The King of kings is drawing near;
> The Saviour of the world is here!

> "Redeemer, come! I open wide
> My heart to Thee, here, Lord, abide.
> Let me Thy inner presence feel;
> Thy grace and love in me reveal."

"Who is the King of Glory"? the song asks on two different occasions. Until we know the answer to that question, we'll never open the gates of our hearts. Until we acknowledge the Lord of Hosts, we'll never let him in.

This was an important point to Handel who was particularly sensitive to *Messiah's* spiritual elements. When after a performance of Messiah Handel was complimented for "providing the town with such a fine entertainment," Handel said, "I should be sorry if I only entertained them; I wished to make them better."

Even in his last years, wracked by disease and blindness, the great composer walked from his home to worship twice a day at St. George's Church.

Combining as he did great religious truth and great art may be the sublime accomplishment, the greatest calling of humankind.

"Lift Up Your Heads, O Ye Gates" takes as its subject nothing less than the greatest being in the universe, the Almighty Creator, the Lord of Hosts, the King of Glory.

And Handel, with God's help, was able to rise to the occasion.

4HIM

"THE TRUMPET SHALL SOUND"

4Him

The trumpet shall sound, and the dead shall be raised incorruptible, and we shall be changed. For this corruptible must put on incorruption, and this mortal must put on immortality.

– 1 Corinthians 15:52–53

4HIM—ANDY CHRISMAN, Mark Harris, Marty Magehee and Kirk Sullivan—have always hit the ground running. Just days after singing with the ever-popular, ever-touring TRUTH, they were signed to the Benson label as a quartet. Their first release, 4HIM's "Where There Is Faith," hit #1 and helped the group win a Dove as Best New Artist for 1991. They've been the Gospel Music Association's Group of the Year the past two years. And in the midst of all of that, they've performed more than two hundred concerts per year and recorded a couple more albums, *Face the Nation* and the best-selling *The Basics of Life*.

You'd think their foray into *The Young Messiah* would be somewhat less stressful—or at least not quite so headlong. But that wasn't the case. According to Chrisman, joining *The Young Messiah* in 1992 boosted the still-new group's visibility and opened new opportunities to be heard by a larger audience.

"We were real excited that first year to be part of the tour," Chrisman said. "It made our year. And now it is almost like a high school reunion each November when the new tour starts and we get to see everybody again.

"I remember our last concert of the tour that first year. After it was over everyone got on the shuttle bus to go back to our hotel. We began swapping telephone numbers and pictures, and saying all those senti-mental things. We'd all gotten so close in the previous weeks that we were like brothers and sisters. Everybody was in tears by the time we got off the bus. A lot of us stayed up a long time in the hotel lobby and talked, shared memories and prayed with each other.

"That's one of the bittersweet things about the tour. You get so close in such a short amount of time, and then it's over and you know that you won't see most of those people for another six to eight months."

Of course, it isn't quite the same with 4HIM as with solo artists. Andy, Mark, Marty and Kirk are best friends and each other's devoted fans.

"We go in with a strength that a lot of people would like to have," Chrisman admitted. "We have each other to go to with our problems and we are accountable to each other. We often share hotel rooms so we have someone to talk to before we go to bed.

"I imagine solo artists live for the summer festivals or *The Young Messiah* tour—there are so few chances to be with other artists. We are fortunate that we all go through the same things on the road, and because we're a group, we've got each other to share it with."

What they share in "The Trumpet Shall Sound" is a musicality and originality that makes the piece a delight for audiences.

"'The Trumpet Shall Sound' is tough to sing because there are only two lines in the whole song, repeated over and over. The challenge was to make those repetitions sound different and to grow and grow until the big finale at the end. And I really like what we did."

So do others. The result is a brilliant piece of work. Under 4HIM's bell-like voices and incomparable harmonies is an urgent, unstoppable musical track, one that surges and recedes like the tide. 4HIM adds its trademark harmonies and vocal twists throughout the singing, swaying music.

"The Trumpet Shall Sound" sounds supremely difficult to reproduce live, but surprisingly Chrisman says that is not the case.

"We don't often do things in the studio that we can't do on stage," he said. "Granted, there are more vocal parts than we could cover live, so we had to put a few of those on tracks. But a lot of it is energy. If we put enough energy into a song it is easier to sing live.

"We love singing `The Trumpet Shall Sound'. We get antsy at concerts waiting to perform that song."

In the original, three-to-four hour *Messiah*, Chrisman said that

> "*Christ returning from the grave and coming back to life, that's what gives us hope. All of the stuff we experience down here, all of the persecutions we're going through, all of the inconsistencies of this life—forget them.*"

"The Trumpet Shall Sound" follows a lengthy section of somber, intro-spective, even sorrowful music.

"That helps create a change of pace when that song comes along in the concert," he said. "The storyline in this part of *Messiah* is really sad. Up to this point we've been singing about how Jesus was beaten, crucified and how everyone left him. I'm literally in tears every night as some of the artists sing.

"But then it gets to this point and we slide in with that lyric, `The trumpet shall sound and the dead shall be RAISED!' Finally, Christ is tri-umphant!

"Christ returning from the grave and coming back to life, that's what gives us hope. All of the stuff we experience down here, all of the persecutions we're going through, all of the inconsistencies of this life—forget them. We're going to be changed into the image of Christ!"

It is a message that Chrisman says people are hungry to hear.

"They need to hear that there's not going to be any more war, or hatred, or pain—we're going to be *changed*," he said.

4HIM recently spent an afternoon with author Max Lucado, who will serve as host/chaplain for the 1994 *Young Messiah* tour.

"Max talked about Romans 8," Chrisman recalled. "He said, `One word appears in this chapter more than any other—*groaning*. There's a lot of groaning going on: creation is groaning, the Holy Spirit is groan-ing, we're groaning. And maybe that's not such a bad thing. Maybe groaning is a gift from God to keep us from becoming content in this life, to aim our lives toward the change that's going to come.

"To me, this middle part of *Messiah* is groaning about what has to happen before we can be changed. Then, `The Hallelujah Chorus' storms in after that—and all heaven breaks loose! That's when the angels become excited and express their joy that Christ is risen and so all of humankind *will* be changed forever.

"It's a moment worth waiting for!"

Chapter 15

TWILA PARIS

"Worthy Is the Lamb That Was Slain"/"Hallelujah"

Twila Paris

Worthy is the Lamb that was slain to receive power, and riches, and wisdom, and strength, and honour, and glory, and blessing . . . Blessing, and honor, and glory, and power, be unto him that sitteth upon the throne, and unto the Lamb, forever and ever.

Hallelujah! for the Lord God omnipotent reigneth. The king-doms of this world are become the kingdoms of our Lord, and

of his Christ; and he shall reign for ever and ever. King of

Kings, and Lord of Lords. Hallelujah!

– Revelation 5:12–13; 19:6; 11:15; 19:16

ALTHOUGH TWILA PARIS HAS BEEN RECORDING well-received albums since 1981, she became an "overnight sensation" only recently. Her latest release, *Beyond a Dream*, was the best-selling contemporary Christian album for most of 1994. She was the Gospel Music Association's Female Vocalist of the Year in '92 and '93. She became a spokesperson for the three-hundred-store Parable Group chain. And on and on.

In sum, in a remarkably short time, Paris has become one of the best-known and best-loved artists in Christian music. And it's no surprise that she now is a fixture on *The Young Messiah* tour.

"The tours have been a good experience for me," she said. "Everybody had been telling me, `Oh, you've got to come out and do this with us—it is so much fun.' So I did.

"We artists are used to being in charge on our own tours. If we're running late, we know they won't leave without us. On this tour, we were all equal members of a team, all following the same rules.

Being on the *Young Messiah* touring bus was another of the highlights for Paris.

"Because all the women were on one bus, it was like a rolling slumber party," she said. "We got a chance to hang out and have good conversations. And we got to know each other really well. Sometimes we sang in sports arenas where there was only a big locker room to dress in. So we girls would all pile in there, borrowing safety pins, eyeliner and clothes steamers."

As is with friends, sometimes the interactions turned into teasing. For instance, late in the tour, Sandi Patty slipped on stage during her song "And the Glory of the Lord." Although she wasn't hurt, Paris said that Sandi's ego was bruised repeatedly in the days that followed!

"BeBe Winans tortured her several times a day—luckily there were only two dates left on the tour," Paris said. "Whenever he'd pass her, he'd adopt this high, squeaky voice and sing, `hath spoken it, hath spoken it!'—the last lines of `And the Glory of the Lord'—and fall down on the ground! Poor Sandi, no one gave her any mercy on that, and she took it with good humor."

There also were plenty of practical jokes played on tour—with several artists fingering Paris as one of the main culprits. Paris sweetly denied any culpability. Well, almost . . .

"There definitely was some practical joking going on," she said innocently, "but that illustrates the kind of camaraderie we had."

But when the music begins, Paris becomes all business. Her featured number in *The Young Messiah*, "Worthy Is the Lamb That Was Slain," is particularly challenging because everyone in the audience is anticipating what's next: the best-known piece in the classical literature, The Hallelujah Chorus.

In "Worthy Is the Lamb," arranger Alan Moore wisely didn't try to compete. The song builds slowly, majestically, emphasizing Paris's solo vocals, playing off the obvious tension of what is to come.

> "It's one thing to talk about the grandeur of God and his majesty. It is quite another to say `Worthy is the Lamb.' That brings worship to a more intimate level."

"It is a worshipful moment," Paris said. "It's one thing to talk about the grandeur of God and his majesty. It is quite another to say `Worthy is the Lamb.' That brings worship to a more intimate level.

"That song leads you to think about your own salvation, the gift

Jesus gave you and what it cost him—`Worthy is the Lamb that was slain and hath redeemed us to God by his blood.'

"Then you move into `to receive power, and riches, and wisdom, and strength, and honor, and glory, and blessing'—that's where it quietly starts building. That's when you start sensing, as the choir comes in, that `The Hallelujah Chorus' is coming!"

Paris remains on stage as the other artists return and the massed choirs begin with the heart-stopping line, "Hallelujah! for the Lord God omnipotent reigneth . . ."

"I believe `The Hallelujah Chorus' is the best worship song ever written," she said. "Handel was anointed to write it.

"I grew up singing it in church and in choirs in school—I've been singing *Messiah* forever! I can remember being in high school choir and singing that song at Christmas time. I never could get through it without tears welling up in my eyes."

Paris said that while she is singing—and listening—to `The Hallelujah Chorus,' she senses the nearness of the Kingdom of God.

"And I have this incredible feeling of being part of it—and of how big it is," she said. "You get a picture of the saints of all the ages singing in heaven around the throne with all the Christians and saints and angels of all time."

> "*When Christians sing `The Hallelujah Chorus' as an act of worship unto the Lord, God receives it. Imagine how many times he's heard it, but I have a feeling he never gets tired of hearing it.*"

"When Christians sing `The Hallelujah Chorus' as an act of worship unto the Lord, God receives it. Imagine how many times he's heard it, but I have a feeling he never gets tired of hearing it.

"I'll be surprised if we don't sing it in heaven!"

Paris says that the arrangement of "The Hallelujah Chorus" definitely fits in a pretty soulful groove. "Then it becomes a very joyous expression of worship. When the dancers arrive at center stage giving it all they've got, it becomes a celebration.

"Then you add BeBe & CeCe wailing, cutting loose and improvising at the end. The structure gives way so that everyone can express their own hearts to the Lord on top of the foundation of `The Hallelujah Chorus.'"

Not that there was ever anything wrong with the original "Hallelujah Chorus," she hastens to add:

"I think it is wonderful to have both the traditional form and the new arrangement."

That brings up the question, Is *Messiah* divinely inspired?

"I believe it," she said. "Handel obviously put himself at God's disposal—and God created through him.

"So there is no doubt in my mind that it was divinely inspired, particularly in light of how quickly it was written."

Inspiration—or heavenly dictation—is something Paris is qualified to speak of. It's evident in her songs some of which include "The Joy of the Lord," "How Beautiful," "Lamb of God," "We Will Glorify" and "He is Exalted."

It is what happens when an artist finishes a song and looks back in amazement and says, "Wow! did I write that?" And the answer is, "No, I didn't."

"Song writing is a craft," Paris said, "but every once in awhile a song comes that goes beyond your craft and it is a gift.

"*Messiah* and Hallelujah Chorus she says, "*definitely* are gifts straight from God!"

Afterword

The Young Messiah is a memorable event, commemorating an even more remarkable event—the birth of Jesus Christ.

But long before the audience arrives, before the curtain rises, the lights come on and the performers appear onstage, there are people working all year behind the scenes to bring about the concert event of the season.

Here are profiles of some of those people.

NORMAN MILLER
EXECUTIVE PRODUCER

It all began more than three decades ago in the tiny Scots village of Hawick, outside Edinburgh, where young Norman Miller was already displaying an interest in all things musical.

"I'd gone with my parents to see *Messiah* every year since I was five years old," Miller recalled. "I knew it by heart. We had a copy that I played all the time on my gramophone."

When Miller later toured with Christian musical groups, he still managed to break away at least once year to see a production of *Messiah*, usually in London.

"I remember thinking—literally twenty years ago—how incredible it would be to do a contemporary version of Handel's *Messiah*," Miller said, "but back then we had neither the artists nor the resources to make it work."

Once Miller started his own company, Proper Management, one of the first projects he pursued was recording *Handel's Young Messiah*.

"That first year we averaged something like 14,000 people a night," he said. And each succeeding tour became more successful. In the first three years, *Performance Magazine* listed it as one of the Top Four tours in the United States in average attendance.

By this time, Miller felt *Young Messiah* needed updating, so he took the concept—on a grander, more heavily arranged scale—to Sparrow Records.

Miller met with Sparrow execs Billy Ray Hearn, Bill Hearn and Peter York. "We came up with a list of the artists we wanted. And everyone we asked agreed to do it," Miller said.

When Sparrow's *New Young Messiah* was released in September 1993, it nearly outsold—in the first quarter alone—the original version's total sales.

Miller attributes that reaction to *Messiah's* rare combination of sacred and classical music, a mix that is acceptable to Christian and non-Christian alike. ("It was the first `crossover' hit!" he adds happily.)

But the success of the 1993 tour doesn't mean that Miller is ready to rest on his laurels.

"The tour is going to continue to change. For instance, in 1994 author Max Lucado is co-hosting with Sandi Patty and narrating the concert.

"And the artists will continue to change. We've added some new artists and expanded the roles of others.

"I don't see where we are now with the *Young Messiah* as a destination. It's just part of the journey. And I'm honored to be along for the ride."

GREG NELSON
PRODUCER

Once Sparrow CEO Billy Ray Hearn and co-executive producers Norman Miller and Sandi Patty agreed on the concept for *The New Young Messiah*, they turned to producer deluxe Greg Nelson.

Nelson, best known as Patty's producer (and a gifted songwriter in his own right), then undertook the unenviable task of coordinating seventeen artists, a dozen arrangers, a trip to London, several choirs, an orchestra, studio musicians, managers, agents, spouses and record labels—meshing them all, and turning out a piece of art in less than ninety days.

But he had a history with *Messiah*. "I have an appreciation and love for the music," he said.

"The tough thing was trying to contemporize a classical gem like *Messiah.*

As the project began to take shape, Nelson quickly knew that something extraordinary was happening. "It was one of the richest times of my life," he said.

Nelson was astonished by some of the performances when he eventually saw the live production of *The Young Messiah.*

"One of the highlights was the trio of Larnelle Harris, Steve Green and Michael English singing `Surely He Hath Borne Our Griefs'," he said.

"And Steve Green singing `I Know That My Redeemer Liveth' . . . I *believed* it when he sang it—Steve puts his life and who he is into that song."

Interestingly, there is a spiritual connection between Handel and Nelson. Handel began losing his eyesight in his final years. Nelson too lost his eyesight—only to have it miraculously restored some time later.

"Passion comes from the difficult parts of our lives," Nelson said.

And in the works of Handel and Nelson—though they be separated by 250 years—there is passion a'plenty.

RALPH CARMICHAEL CONDUCTOR

It must be comforting for today's top Christian artists to look down from the stage while singing *The Young Messiah* and see the dean of contemporary Christian music conducting the orchestra.

Few of the artists were born when Ralph Carmichael began his long career in religious music. But even from the beginning his was more than just a career; it has been a musical crusade to put the timeless Message into music and idiom of the people.

His early youth musicals (*Tell It Like It Is, Natural High*), his gift of song writing ("He's Everything to Me," "New 23rd"), his leadership as president of the innovative Light Records (Andrae Crouch, Allies), even his scoring for the early Billy Graham films (*The Restless Ones, His Land*), have marked

Carmichael as a pioneer in an industry noted more for settlers and farmers.

Were it not for the efforts of Carmichael, Sparrow CEO Billy Ray Hearn and other visionaries like them, there might not *be* a *Young Messiah*.

"One of my early choir jobs was as minister of music at Temple Baptist Church in downtown Los Angeles in the 1950s," Carmichael said. "I had heard the Hallelujah Chorus—that was the extent of my musical knowledge of Handel.

"But we performed *Messiah* one Christmas with fifty musicians from the Los Angeles Philharmonic and a 200-voice 'All-Baptist Choir.' I was scared to death, but I never got over my love for the music."

In the early '60s, Carmichael's gift for orchestration and original composition found him busy scoring for motion pictures. It was during recording the soundtrack of *His Land* that he conceived of updating the Hallelujah Chorus to a rock beat.

Carmichael said he didn't think much about *Messiah* after that until early 1989 when Norman Miller called and asked him to conduct *Handel's Young Messiah*. Carmichael conducted the orchestra and choir on the first tour and hasn't missed a performance since.

"But every night when we hit that Hallelujah Chorus, it's goose-bump time. I get caught up in it just like the audience."

You only have to be around him for a while before that kind of enthusiasm is contagious. Carmichael's presence on the tour has meant an entire new generation of Christian musicians has gotten to know the man with the rakish, debonair white mustache.

"What a thrill it is to get acquainted with today's top artists," he said. "They're all absolutely precious to me and I feel like a granddaddy to them all."

But after ninety-two performances, has the music lost its freshness?

"There's nothing boring about *Messiah* musically," he said. "It is a fabulous work that has stood the test of time.

"I don't know why this work is more popular than about anything else. But it is about a subject that changed our universe—the first advent of Christ, and the foretelling of all these prophecies. It is all Scripture—every word—and people respond to God's Word.

"Now couple that with some of the most gorgeous melody lines and most fantastic rhythmic lines and chordal developments in all of music—and you've got something!"

But then, Christian music could say the same thing about a national treasure like Ralph Carmichael!

TOBIN JONES
DANCER/CHOREOGRAPHER

It is a thrilling moment in *The Young Messiah* tour. As the familiar, pulse-pounding strains of the Hallelujah Chorus begin, the audience automatically, almost instinctively, surges to its feet. From the side entrances one of the most glittering arrays of talent in contemporary Christian music ever assembled files in together, joining the massed choirs in the refrain.

And then, spinning to the center of the stage, is a blur of white, a whirling dancer whose every step, every movement, amplifies the soaring music.

The dancer is Tobin James. Her inspired movements are a combination of African-American dance, classical ballet, interpretive jazz and moving, shifting, shimmering body language. They become the centerpoint, the visual focal point of the massive "Chorus," which by now contains far more singers, musicians and elements for the eye to assimilate.

Suddenly, a second dancer joins Tobin. Together they complete a tightly choreographed spirit dance, two angels lost in a celestial praise chorus, barely able to contain the joy of the Incarnation.

As Gloria Gaither says, "Tobin dances the song my soul would sing if it could soar. No wonder the psalmist commands people of God to rejoice in him who made them and to 'praise his name in the dance . . . for the Lord takes pleasure in his people'" (Ps. 149).

Not surprisingly, the artist behind the boldly beautiful, visually arresting praise dance is a soft-spoken, deeply committed Christian. Tobin James graduated from the famed Philadelphia College of Performing Arts in 1985 with a Bachelor of Fine Arts degree in dance. For several years she danced professionally, a graceful, lithe figure spiraling across stages in the Northeast. But always, no matter how prestigious the venue, something kept nagging at her heart.

"I always wanted to dance for the Lord, but thought that I needed to make it in the mainstream industry first—as validation.

"But one day, I felt the Lord asking me if I could be satisfied without ever having that validation. I said yes."

James vowed from then on to dance only for the Lord and went to work for a company called Here's Life Intercity. It wasn't long before James attracted the attention of Steve Green who added her to his concert for the holidays.

Word of James's sensitive, impassioned performances quickly spread. She soon became a familiar figure to audiences, performing with Bill and Gloria Gaither, including a memorable evening at the Christian Artists Music Seminars in Estes Park, Colorado.

"Interestingly enough," James said, "my husband had seen an advertisement for *Handel's Young Messiah* even before that and said, `You should dance for that.' By then, I had quit trying to create my own opportunities, so I said, `If the Lord wants it, I'll be there.'

"Sure enough, a couple of months later, Norman Miller asked me to dance for *The Young Messiah* tour.

"I had by then decided that the Lord was the only reason for me to dance. Whatever I did had to be something that could point people to the Lord or a way for me to express my love for him."

James, who joined *The Young Messiah* tour in its second season and has been a staple ever since, said what she treasures most about the production has been the interaction with her fellow artists.

"What I remember are the characters among the singers and musicians," she said. "Everyone always has been wonderful. There is a lot of mutual respect among the artists."

James had only heard Hallelujah Chorus once before joining the cast of *The Young Messiah* and even then as a small girl in church it made her cry.

"I also remember wanting to dance to it even back then," she said. "It amazes me that years later I *am* dancing to it."

With the incredible array of talented musicians and singers, what *does* dance add to the Hallelujah Chorus? "I would say it's victory," James said with quiet conviction. "It's not just hearing it, it's *seeing* it. You're seeing someone dancing the victory she's found in Jesus."

*The Concert Event
of the Decade
is now available on*

HOME VIDEO

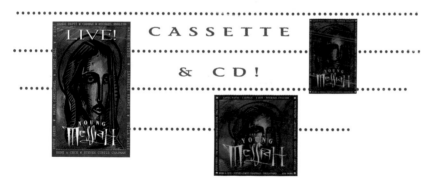

CASSETTE

& CD!

CHECK YOUR LOCAL CHRISTIAN BOOKSTORE FOR THESE AND

OTHER OUTSTANDING MUSIC, VIDEO AND BOOK PRODUCTS FROM SPARROW.

*W*ORLD VISION IS AN INTERNATIONAL CHRISTIAN RELIEF AND DEVELOPMENT AGENCY INTENT ON HELPING THE WORLD'S POOR BY MEETING THEIR IMMEDIATE NEEDS AND EQUIPPING THEM TO MEET THEIR OWN FUTURE NEEDS.

WORLD VISION

P.O. BOX 1131 • PASADENA, CA 91131-0151
1 (800) 432-4200
KAYM4B